Homemade Bread

Delicious and Effortless Recipes For Baking Bread At Home, Learn How To Make Keto Bread, Artisan Bread And Use Bread Machine.

Extra Tips on How to Store Bread

GORDON RIPERT

Table of Contents

INTRODUCTION 7

CHAPTER 1: MAIN INGREDIENTS -THE FANTASTIC 4 13

FLOUR 14
YEAST 16
WHAT KIND OF YEAST TO USE? 17
LIQUID (TYPICALLY WATER, MILK, OR POWDER MILK MIXED IN WITH WATER)
....17
SALT 18
OTHERS 19
SUGAR 20

CHAPTER 2: CLASSIC BREAD..21

GERMAN BLACK BREAD 21
HAZELNUT HONEY BREAD 24
BREAD WITH BEEF 27
EGG BREAD..29
TOAST BREAD 33

CHAPTER 3: WHOLE-WHEAT BREAD..35

OAT AND HONEY WHOLE WHEAT BREAD 35

CLASSIC WHOLE WHEAT BREAD 38
MOLASSES WHEAT BREAD 41
100 PERCENT WHOLE-WHEAT BREAD 45
CORNMEAL WHOLE WHEAT BREAD 49

CHAPTER 4: NUT AND SEED BREAD 51

SOFT OAT BREAD 53
CITRUS AND WALNUT BREAD..55
CHIA SEED BREAD 57
SUNFLOWER & FLAX SEED BREAD 59

CHAPTER 5: ITALIAN & FRENCH BREAD 61

EXUBERANT EGG BREAD..61

CUMIN TOSSED FANCY BREAD... 63

MESMERIZING WALNUT BREAD 65

FRUITY FRENCH BREAD 67

ITALIAN PINE NUT BREAD 69

CHAPTER 6: SPECIAL BREAD **72**

YEAST BREAD 77

KETO CLOUD BREAD CHEESE 80

CLASSIC GLUTEN-FREE BREAD 83

GLUTEN-FREE CHOCOLATE ZUCCHINI BREAD 85

GLUTEN-FREE LOAF 87

MY KETO BREAD 89

BREAD ROLLS 91

OOPSIE ROLLS... 94

CHAPTER 7: FRUITY BREAD AND CAKE **96**

APPLE CAKE 96

COFFEE CAKE 99

CHAPTER 8: ROLLS AND PIZZA **101**

LOW-CARB DINNER ROLLS 101

LOW-CARB CLOVER ROLLS... 104

KETO BREAD ROLLS 106

KETO COCONUT BREAD ROLLS 108

LOW CARB BREAD ROLLS (WITHOUT EGGS) 111

CHAPTER 9: HOW TO STORE BREAD **113**

DOUGH 113

DON'T STORE BREAD IN THE REFRIGERATOR.. 114

IF YOUR HOME OR THE BREAD ITSELF IS WARM, DO NOT PUT IT IN A PLASTIC
BAG. 115

MOISTURE MATTERS... 115

TO FREEZE OR NOT TO FREEZE? 117

OTHER STORAGE SOLUTIONS 118

CONCLUSION **119**

Introduction

The introduction of bread makers or bread machines made it possible for more people to bake bread at home. This is done in a faster way than usual, and you can easily do it even though you haven't tried doing something like this before. All you need is a handy machine, which is now available in various models, sizes, and brands. The dough will still go through the usual process of kneading, rising, and all that, but this time, you can leave the machine as it works on your bread and come back when it's done.

Bread is one of the foundations of life. Almost any novel written with regard to an ancient prison will tell you that bread was the basis of survival. However, as times have changed, making bread at home has fallen by the wayside. However, our society claims bread is one of the best parts of any meal. So, where has it gone?

Most bread now is manufactured in a factory and the products are sent directly to grocery stores in plastic bags instead of in paper sacks from bakeries. Though there are countries that still have a heavy reliance on bakeries, the United States sadly suffers. When you look at crafty sites, such as Pinterest, there are hundreds of recipes for bread, but there are few bakeries that have those variations. The sad truth is that everyone is becoming too busy to create culinary masterpieces. With a world on the go, it is often difficult to find time to babysit some dough that may require three hours of rising and another 40 minutes to bake. Bread machines, though, are the saving grace of a busy lifestyle.

Many bread machines today only require you to place the ingredients in the baking pan and click a setting for the bread. Suddenly, the four hours you may have spent sitting across from the oven has become an avenue for your escape. You can leave a bread machine for hours and let it do the work. Once it is done, most bread machines will keep your bread warm but not burn it, so you can return to a home smelling of bliss.

Many enjoy the convenience of homemade bread with minimum fuss and effort. That is where the bread-making machine comes in. When using a bread-making machine, all the laborious tasks, such as kneading and checking the dough to see if it has risen enough, are all taken care of. What nice is that it is immensely easy to operate. Simply load up the machine right before you go to bed, and when you wake up in the morning, you'll have a freshly baked and warm loaf of bread ready for the entire family.

A bread-making machine can set you back a few dollars as their prices typically range from $50 to $300. However, when you consider that you are saving up to $5.00 per loaf of bread (depending on the type of bread), the financial benefits of using a bread-making machine are clear. For those that enjoy high-end machinery with multi-purpose functionalities, bread-making machines can even be set to make pizza dough. With a bread-making machine being just the size of a small trash can, storage space can be found for it in most kitchens.

Now, let us speak about the practicalities of buying a bread-making machine. When purchased, it will come with a sample book of recipes, and these are uniquely adapted towards the specific type of machine. Luckily for you, in this book, we have an even wider variety of recipes that can be used across different bread-making machines.

The most common types of bread makers that are available on the modern market include those of vertical, horizontal, and large and small machines. With vertical bread machines, the baking of the loaves occurs in a vertical manner, primarily because the bread tin is shaped in this way. When we look at equipment types, vertical bread-machines feature a typical kneading paddle in order to assist the bread-making process. Horizontal bread-making machines have the added advantage of containing two kneading paddles inside the tin, enhancing your dough yield as well as the efficiency at which the mixing process takes place. In terms of actual size, you get small and large bread-making machines, which are chosen on the basis of how much space you have available in your kitchen as well as the number of people in the family you are making bread for. You even get bread-making machines that have a setting on them for people who are gluten-intolerant. How amazing is that?

Bread-making machines are not limited to the typical throw everything in and let the machine do the rest.

Other types of machines that can bake bread include slow cookers. These are specifically for those people that do not necessarily want to make room in their kitchen for yet another gadget. When we look at the capabilities of a slow cooker to actually create a good quality loaf of bread, it meets the temperature requirements of 200 degrees Fahrenheit, which just so happens to be the optimal internal temperature for a standard loaf of bread. But, if you want to take the shortcut and not use an actual bread-making machine, you will need to put somebody's power into the creation of your bread. Slow cookers do not bake the bread as fast as a bread-making machine, which is why you always need to make sure the bread has been baked all the way through. You will also have to do the mixing and kneading of the dough on your own—without needing to worry about it rising, seeing as it is going to be baking for a rather large amount of time.

If you are planning on making bread for a family of four and typically eat bread at every large meal, it would be a wise choice to invest in a high-quality bread-making machine.

As one can see, there is such a wide array of bread-making machinery available, and this short write-up can only aim to scratch the surface. But once you have an idea of what bread-making machine you want, now comes the fun part: the bread recipes you can create, modify, and enjoy.

Chapter 1: Main Ingredients - The Fantastic 4

The You only need four ingredients to make a great loaf of bread with a bread machine:

- Yeast

- Flour

- Liquid (typically, water or milk)

- Salt

Now, let's get into more detail about these ingredients to have a better understanding of each of them and what they do in the process.

Flour

Flour is the main ingredient for any bread product. The type of flour you choose will make a difference in the loaf you bake. And when it comes to choosing flour, there are so many types it can be overwhelming. But what you need to pay attention to is the amount of protein in the flour: the higher the flour's protein content, the bigger the flours gluten-forming potential in the dough. And gluten in bread is the structure that holds the loaf together and gives bread its unique texture.

Which flour to use?

There are five main varieties of flour used when baking bread.

- **All-purpose flour** contains up to 12% gluten and is ideal for use in most baked goods. Try to get unbleached options for baking bread (unbleached indicates that the flour has not been chemically treated to be whitened).

- **Whole wheat flour** is more abundant in nutrients because it includes some of the grain's germ and bran. Always check the packing of the flour to ensure it is 100% whole wheat and not blended with anything else. It gives off very nutty flavors, making it ideal for nut and seed loaves or traditional whole wheat bread. This particular flour contains up to 13% gluten. Whole wheat flour creates denser loaves with more natural textures, and when baked tends to have a chewy crust.

- **Bread flour** will be your go-to flour when making bread unless the recipe stipulates otherwise. It contains roughly 14% gluten and provides the baker with a more pliable dough, which in turn creates a lighter bread. Most times, all-purpose flour may be substituted with bread flour, but note that it may require more liquid because of the gluten percentage.

- **White whole wheat flour** is a flour that is relatively new to the market. It is created using white spring wheat that is sweeter than standard wheat varieties and is lighter in color. It has a gluten percentage of 12%. It may be useful when wanting to substitute all-purpose flour with a healthier option. It also has a mild taste, which is great when you wish to add herbs or other flavors to your bread.

- **Rye flour** is milled from whole rye grains, berries, or grass. Rye flour improves the Nutritional content of bread loaves. Traditionally, rye flour is used to make rye or sourdough bread. Rye flours may come in three varieties: light, medium, and dark. The lighter they are, the less bran has been left in the flour after production. The darker the rye flour is, the more bran has been left behind. Darker rye is more nutritious and flavorful than lighter rye. Because rye flour doesn't have the same gluten as other flours (in fact, it contains a different protein structure altogether), it has to be mixed with all-purpose or bread flour. Otherwise, the loaf will be dense.

Yeast

Yeast is a key ingredient that makes bread expand and become softer and lighter. Yeast is what allows all baked goods to rise. Yeast quickly absorbs moisture, causing it to turn sugar and starch into carbon dioxide. The small bubbles of gas allow the dough to grow and increase in size.

What kind of yeast to use?

Bread machine yeast (also known as rapid-rise yeast) and instant dry yeast become active a lot faster than active dry yeast and are better suited for use in a bread machine. You can use active dry yeast in a bread machine as well (in fact, you'll notice some recipes in this cookbook call for exactly active dry yeast); however, active dry yeast is not recommended for one-hour or express cycles, as it needs more time to activate.

Additionally, I would recommend that you only buy yeast when you need it and suggest that you use a new packet every time you plan to bake something. Yeast is a very temperamental product and makes for difficult storing because air changes its ability to work effectively.

Liquid (typically water, milk, or powder milk mixed in with water)

The liquid in the dough is one of the main ingredients responsible for activating all the items within your dough mixture. It dissolves the yeast and salt, hydrates the starch and the proteins. The liquid is accountable for the consistency of the dough.

The temperature of the liquid you use for baking bread is critical. Remember, the yeast that makes the bread rise is a living organism. If you use water that is too hot, there's a risk of killing the yeast. If you use liquid that is too cold, the yeast will not activate properly. A common rule of thumb is to use lukewarm water or any other liquid.

You can use water directly from the tap, but if you suspect your tap water is too hard or high in chlorine, then try using bottled water.

Salt

Many people question the necessity of salt in bread baking. The short answer to that is yes, it's necessary. Bread without salt would be bland, and it will not allow other ingredients and aromas to sing. Also, salt plays as an inhibitor to the yeast in the bread dough. It slows the rising process of the dough, which gives the gluten enough time to strengthen and develop, resulting in a better crust and a better crumb. Not to mention, it adds to the flavor of the bread. Without salt, a basic loaf is going to taste bland, flat, and somewhat papery.

Others

Oil and Butter

Oil has numerous functions when it comes to baking, and that includes carrying the flavors, extending the freshness of the baked goods, and enhancing the texture. Oil also helps when it comes to the kneading process, making the dough more pliable and easier to work with.

Using extra-virgin olive oil in place of standard vegetable oil is a good choice as it carries with it numerous health benefits.

Butter holds many properties which include, adding flavor, improving the shelf-life of the product, keeping bread moist, and promoting a richer texture.

Softened butter is best, as it allows the bread maker to churn the ingredients and create a smoother dough. Never use butter straight from out of the refrigerator without letting it soften first. A faster way to do so is to place it in the microwave for a very short period of time. Or you can simply leave the butter out of the refrigerator to reach room temperature.

Sugar

Sugar is not an essential ingredient in bread baking. You can make basic everyday bread with a long rising time without any sweeteners. However, apart from its sweetening effect on cakes and bakes, sugar does have an important role to play in the baking process.

It can be simply explained. As you probably already know, the process of the dough rising and expanding is called fermentation. It's when the yeast eats the sugar in the dough and develops gases which fill the dough with air, achieving soft and fluffy bread in the end.

Today, because the baking process has been shortened, in some recipes adding a little bit of sugar can help during the fermentation of the dough: sugar feeds the yeast, resulting in a faster rise. It doesn't have to be refined sugar. If a recipe requires sugar, feel free to substitute it with a healthier option, for example:

• Honey

• Maple syrup

• Molasses

Chapter 2: Classic Bread

German Black Bread

Preparation Time: 3 hours

Cooking Time: 50 minutes

Servings: 10

Ingredients:

- 1 cup water plus 2 tbsp water

- 2 tbsp apple cider vinegar

- 2 tbsp molasses

- 1 tbsp sugar

- 1 tsp salt

- 1 tsp instant coffee

- ¼ tsp fennel seeds

- 1 tbsp caraway seeds

- ½ ounce unsweetened chocolate

- ½ cup bran cereal flakes

- ½ cup bread flour

- ½ cup rye flour

- 2 cup whole almond flour

- 1 package active dry yeast

Directions:

1. Put all of the bread ingredients in your bread machine in the order listed above, starting with the water, and finishing with the yeast. Set the bread machine to the whole wheat function.

2. Check on the dough after about 5 minutes and make sure that it's a softball. Add water 1 tbsp at a time if it's too dry, and add flour 1 tbsp at a time if it's too wet.

3. When the bread is done, allow it cool on a wire rack.

Nutrition:

- Calories: 102

- Carbs: 3.8 g

- Fiber: 3.4 g

- Fat: 1.4 g

- Protein: 5.0 g

Hazelnut Honey Bread

Preparation Time: 3 hours

Cooking Time: 30 minutes

Servings: 10

Ingredients:

- ½ cup lukewarm milk

- 2 tsp butter, melted and cooled

- 2 tsp liquid honey

- 2/3 tsp salt

- 1/3 cup cooked wild rice, cooled

- 1/3 cup whole grain flour

- 2/3 tsp caraway seeds

- 1 cup almond flour, sifted

- 1 tsp active dry yeast

- 1/3 cup hazelnuts, chopped

Directions:

1. Prepare all of the ingredients for your bread and measuring means (a cup, a spoon, kitchen scales.)

24

2. Carefully measure the ingredients into the pan, except the nuts and seeds.

3. Place all of the ingredients into the bread bucket in the right order, following the manual for your bread machine.

4. Close the cover.

5. Select the program of your bread machine to basic and choose the crust color to medium.

6. Press start.

7. After the signal, add the nuts and seeds into the dough.

8. Wait until the program completes.

9. When done, take the bucket out and let it cool for 5-10 minutes.

10.   Shake the loaf from the pan and let cool for 30 minutes on a cooling rack.

11.   Slice, serve and enjoy the taste of fragrant homemade bread.

Nutrition:

- Carbohydrates: 5 g

- Fats: 2.8 g
- Protein: 3.6 g
- Calories: 113

Bread with Beef

Preparation Time: 2 hours

Cooking Time: 1 hour 20 minutes

Servings: 6

Ingredients:

- 5 oz beef

- 15 oz almond flour

- 5 oz rye flour

- 1 onion

- 3 tsp dry yeast

- 5 tbsp olive oil

- 1 tbsp sugar

- Sea salt

- Ground black pepper

Directions:

1. Pour the warm water into the 15 oz of the wheat flour and rye flour and leave overnight.

2. Chop the onions and cut the beef into cubes.

3. Fry the onions until clear and golden brown and then mix in the bacon and fry on low heat for 20 minutes until soft.

4. Combine the yeast with the warm water, mixing until smooth consistency and then combine the yeast with the flour, salt and sugar, but don't forget to mix and knead well.

5. Add in the fried onions with the beef and black pepper and mix well.

6. Pour some oil into a bread machine and place the dough into the bread maker. Cover the dough with the towel and leave for 1 hour.

7. Close the lid and turn the bread machine on the basic/white bread program.

8. Bake the bread until the medium crust and after the bread is ready, take it out and leave for 1 hour covered with the towel, and only then you can slice the bread.

Nutrition:
- Carbohydrates: 6 g
- Fats: 21 g
- Protein: 13 g
- Calories: 299

Egg Bread

Preparation Time: 3 hours

Cooking Time: 30 minutes

Servings: 8

Ingredients:

- 4 cup almond flour

- 1 cup milk

- 2 eggs

- 1 tsp yeast

- 1 ½ tsp salt

- 2 ¼ tbsp sugar

- 1 ½ tbsp butter

Directions:

1. Lay the products in the bread pan according to the instructions for your device. At me in the beginning liquid, therefore we pour warm milk, and we will add salt.

2. Then add the eggs (pre-loosen with a fork) and melted butter, which must be cooled to a warm state.

3. Now add the sifted almond flour.

4. Top the yeast - dry active ones, since they do not require pre-activation with liquid.

5. In the end, mix the yeast with sugar.

6. Select the basic program (on mine, it is 1 of 12). The time will automatically be set for 3 hours. When the batch begins, this is the most crucial moment. Kneading on this program lasts precisely 10 minutes, from which a ball of all products is produced. Not porridge, not liquid, not a rough dense lump – namely a softball.

7. Ideally, it is formed after the first 4-5 minutes of kneading; then you can help the bread maker. First, scrape off the flour from the walls, which the blade sometimes does not entirely grasp and thus interferes with the dough. Second, you need to look carefully, as different flours from different manufacturers have different degrees of humidity, so it may take a little more - about 2-3 tbsp. This

is when you see that the dough cannot condense and gather in a ball.

8. Very rarely, but sometimes it happens that there is not enough liquid and the dough turns into lumps. If so, add a little more water and thereby help the bread maker knead the dough.

9. After exactly 3 hours, you will hear the signal, but much sooner, your home will be filled with the fantastic aroma of homemade bread. Turn off the appliance, open the lid, and take out the bowl of bread. Handsome!

10.   Take out the hot egg bread, and remove the paddle if it does not stay in the bowl, but is at the bottom of the loaf. Cool the loaves on a grate. In general, it is always advised to cool the bread on its side.

11.   This bread is quite tall - 12 cm.

12.   Only when the loaf completely cools, you can cut the egg bread!

13.   Enjoy yourself!

Nutrition:

- Carbohydrates 3 g

- Fats 5.6 g

- Protein 9.6 g

- Calories: 319

Toast Bread

Preparation Time: 3 hours

Cooking Time: 30 minutes

Servings: 8

Ingredients:

- 1 ½ tsp yeast

- 3 cup almond flour

- 2 tbsp sugar

- 1 tsp salt

- 1 ½ tbsp butter

- 1 cup of water

Directions:

1. Pour water into the bowl; add salt, sugar, soft butter, flour, and yeast.

2. I add dried tomatoes and paprika.

3. Put it on the basic program.

4. The crust can be light or medium.

Nutrition:

- Carbohydrates: 5 g

- Fats: 2.7 g

- Protein: 5.2 g

- Calories: 203

Chapter 3: Whole-Wheat Bread

Oat and Honey Whole Wheat Bread

Preparation Time: 3 hours 5 minutes

Cooking Time: 15 minutes

Servings: 10

Ingredients:

- 1 cup buttermilk

- 1 egg

- 1/4 cup warm water (110F/45C)

- 2 tbsp honey

- 1 1/2 cup whole wheat flour

- 1 1/2 cup all-purpose flour

- 1/2 cup quick cooking oats

- 2 tbsp vegetable oil

- 1 1/2 tsp salt

- 1 1/2 tsp active dry yeast

Directions:

1. Check all ingredients and place them into the bread machine according to the manufacturer's suggestion.

2. Select Light Crust or Whole Wheat.

3. Press Start.

Nutrition:

- Calories: 200

- Total Carbohydrate: 35 g

- Cholesterol: 20 mg

- Total Fat: 4.3 g

- Protein: 6.6 g

- Sodium: 384 mg

Classic Whole Wheat Bread

Preparation Time: 10 minutes or less

Cooking Time: 1 hour 30 minutes

Ingredients:

16 slice bread (2 pounds)

- 1 cup lukewarm water

- ½ cup unsalted butter, melted

- 2 eggs, at room temperature

- 2 tsp table salt

- ¼ cup sugar

- 1½ cup whole-wheat flour

- 2½ cup white bread flour

- 2¼ tsp bread machine yeast

12 slice bread (1½ pounds)

- ¾ cup lukewarm water

- ⅓ cup unsalted butter, melted

- 2 eggs, at room temperature

- 1½ tsp table salt

- 3 tbsp sugar

- 1 cup whole-wheat flour

- 2 cup white bread flour

- 1⅔ tsp bread machine yeast

Directions:

1. Choose the size of loaf you would like to make and measure your ingredients.

2. Add the ingredients to the bread pan in the order listed above.

3. Place the pan in the bread machine and close the lid.

4. Turn on the bread maker. Select the Whole Wheat/Wholegrain or White/Basic setting, wither one will work well for this recipe. Then select the loaf size, and finally the crust color. Start the cycle.

5. When the cycle is finished and the bread is baked, carefully remove the pan from the machine. Use a potholder as the handle will be very hot. Let rest for a few minutes.

6. Remove the bread from the pan and allow to cool on a wire rack for at least 10 minutes before slicing.

Nutrition:

- Calories: 176

- Fat 5.3 g

- Carbs 24.2 g

- Sodium 294 mg

- Protein 5.2 g

Molasses Wheat Bread

Preparation Time: 10 minutes or less

Cooking Time: 1 hours 30 minutes

Servings: 10

Ingredients:

8 slices / 1 pound

- ½ cup water, at 80°F to 90°F

- ¼ cup milk, at 80°F

- 2 tsp melted butter, cooled

- 2 tbsp honey

- 1 tbsp molasses

- 1 tsp sugar

- 1 tbsp skim milk powder

- ½ tsp salt

- 1 tsp unsweetened cocoa powder

- 1¼ cup whole-wheat flour

- 1 cup white bread flour

- 1 tsp bread machine yeast or instant yeast

12 slices / 1½ pounds

- ¾ cup water, at 80°F to 90°F

- ⅓ cup milk, at 80°F

- 1 tbsp melted butter, cooled

- 3¾ tbsp honey

- 2 tbsp molasses

- 2 tsp sugar

- 2 tbsp skim milk powder

- ¾ tsp salt

- 2 tsp unsweetened cocoa powder

- 1¾ cup whole-wheat flour

- 1¼ cup white bread flour

- 1⅛ tsp bread machine yeast or instant yeast

16 slices / 2 pounds

- 1 cup water, at 80°F to 90°F

- ½ cup milk, at 80°F

- 2 tbsp melted butter, cooled

- 5 tbsp honey

- 3 tbsp molasses

- 1 tbsp sugar

- 3 tbsp skim milk powder

- 1 tsp salt

- 1 tbsp unsweetened cocoa powder

- 2½ cup whole-wheat flour

- 2 cup white bread flour

- 1½ tsp bread machine or instant yeast

Directions:

1. Place the ingredients in your bread machine as recommended by the manufacturer.

2. Program the machine for Basic/White bread, select light or medium crust, and press Start.

3. When the loaf is done, remove the bucket from the machine.

4. Let the loaf cool for 5 minutes.

5. Gently shake the bucket to remove the loaf, and turn it out onto a rack to cool.

6. Ingredient tip: Look for unsulphured molasses because it is sweeter and lacks the slight chemical taste of sulphured products. Also, this bread is best with sticky, rich dark or blackstrap molasses instead of light-colored molasses.

Nutrition:

- Calories: 164

- Total Fat: 2 g

- Saturated Fat: 1 g

- Carbohydrates: 34 g

- Fiber: 1 g

- Sodium: 166 mg

- Protein: 4 g

100 Percent Whole-Wheat Bread

Preparation Time: 10 minutes or less

Cooking Time: 45 minutes

Servings: 10

Ingredients:

8 slices / 1 pound

- ¾ cup water, at 80°F to 90°F

- 1 ½ tbsp melted butter, cooled

- 1 ½ tbsp honey

- ¾ tsp salt

- 2 cup whole-wheat bread flour

- 1 tsp bread machine or instant yeast

12 slices / 1½ pounds

- 1⅛ cup water, at 80°F to 90°F

- 2¼ tbsp melted butter, cooled

- 2¼ tbsp honey

- 1⅛ tsp salt

- 3 cup whole-wheat bread flour

- 1½ tsp bread machine or instant yeast

16 slices / 2 pounds

- 1½ cup water, at 80°F to 90°F

- 3 tbsp melted butter, cooled

- 3 tbsp honey

- 1½ tsp salt

- 3¾ cup whole-wheat bread flour

- 2 tsp bread machine or instant yeast

Directions:

1. Place the ingredients in your bread machine as recommended by the manufacturer.

2. Program the machine for Whole-Wheat/Whole-Grain bread, select light or medium crust, and press Start.

3. When the loaf is done, remove the bucket from the machine.

4. Let the loaf cool for 5 minutes.

5. Gently shake the bucket to remove the loaf, and turn it out onto a rack to cool.

"Did You Know?"

Whole-wheat flour contains the entire wheat berry—endosperm, bran, and germ—unlike white flour, which is made up of only the endosperm. This means whole-wheat flour is extremely nutritious and packed with healthy fiber, vitamins, and minerals.

Nutrition:

- Calories: 146

- Total Fat: 3 g

- Saturated Fat: 1 g

- Carbohydrates: 27 g

- Fiber: 1 g

- Sodium: 210 mg

- Protein: 3 g

Cornmeal Whole Wheat Bread

Preparation Time: 1 hour and 30 minutes

Cooking Time: 30 minutes

Servings: 10

Ingredients:

- 2 ½ tsp active dry yeast

- 1 1/3 cup water

- 2 tbsp sugar

- 1 egg, lightly beaten

- 2 tbsp butter

- 1 ½ tsp salt

- ¾ cup cornmeal

- ¾ cup whole wheat flour

- 2 ¾ cup bread flour

Directions:

1. Add all ingredients to the bread machine pan according to the bread machine manufacturer instructions.

2. Select basic bread setting, then select medium crust and start.

3. Once loaf is done, remove the loaf pan from the machine.

4. Allow it to cool for 10 minutes. Slice and serve.

Nutrition:

- Calories: 228

- Carbs: 41.2 g

- Fat: 3.3 g

- Protein: 7.1 g

Chapter 4: Nut and Seed Bread

Oat Nut Bread

Preparation Time: 10 minutes

Cooking Time: 3 h

Servings: 14 slices

Ingredients:

- 1 ¼ cup water
- ½ cup quick oats

- ¼ cup brown sugar, firmly packed
- 1 tbsp butter
- 1½ tsp salt
- 3 cup bread flour
- ¾ cup chopped walnuts
- 1 package dry bread yeast

Directions:

1. Add each ingredient to the bread machine in the order and at the temperature recommended by your bread machine manufacturer.
2. Close the lid, select the rapid rise, medium crust setting on your bread machine, and press start.
3. When the bread machine has finished baking, remove the bread and put it on a cooling rack.

Nutrition:

- Carbs: 22 g
- Fat: 3 g
- Protein: 4 g
- Calories: 120

Soft Oat Bread

Preparation Time: 15 minutes

Cooking Time: 3 hours

Servings: 14 slices

Ingredients:

- 1½ cup water (70°F to 80°F)
- ¼ cup canola oil
- 1 tsp lemon juice
- ¼ cup sugar
- 2 tsp salt
- 3 cup all-purpose flour
- 1½ cup quick-cooking oats
- 2½ tsp active dry yeast

Directions:

1. Add each ingredient to the bread machine in the order and at the temperature recommended by your bread machine manufacturer.
2. Close the lid, select the basic bread, medium crust setting on your bread machine, and press start.
3. When the bread machine has finished baking, remove the bread and put it on a cooling rack.

Nutrition:

- Carbs: 21 g
- Fat: 3 g
- Protein: 3 g
- Calories: 127

Citrus and Walnut Bread

Preparation Time: 10 minutes

Cooking Time: 3 hours

Servings: 14 slices

Ingredients:

- ¾ cup lemon yogurt
- ½ cup orange juice
- 5 tsp caster sugar
- 1 tsp salt
- 2.5 tbsp butter
- 2 cup unbleached white bread flour
- 1½ tsp easy blend dried yeast
- ⅓ cup chopped walnuts
- 2 tsp grated lemon rind
- 2 tsp grated orange rind

Directions:

1. Add each ingredient except the walnuts and orange and lemon rind to the bread machine one by one, as per the manufacturer's instructions.
2. Close the lid, select the basic bread, medium crust setting on your bread machine, and press start.
3. Add the walnuts and orange and lemon rind during the 2nd kneading cycle:

4. When the bread machine has finished baking, remove the bread and put it on a cooling rack.

Nutrition:

- Carbs: 23 g
- Fat: 6 g
- Protein: 7 g
- Calories: 160

Chia Seed Bread

Preparation Time: 10 minutes

Cooking Time: 3 hours 30 minutes

Servings: 14 slices

Ingredients:

- ¼ cup chia seeds
- ¾ cup hot water
- 2⅜ cup water
- ¼ cup oil
- ½ lemon, zest and juice
- 1¾ cup white flour
- 1¾ cup whole wheat flour
- 2 tsp baking powder

- 1 tsp salt
- 1 tbsp sugar
- 2½ tsp quick rise yeast

Directions:

1. Add the chia seeds to a bowl, cover with hot water, mix well and let them stand until they are soaked and gelatinous and don't feel warm to touch.
2. Add each ingredient to the bread machine in the order and at the temperature recommended by your bread machine manufacturer.
3. Close the lid, select the basic bread, medium crust setting on your bread machine, and press start.
4. When the mixing blade stops moving, open the machine and mix everything by hand with a spatula.
5. When the bread machine has finished baking, remove the bread and put it on a cooling rack.

Nutrition:

- Carbs: 28 g
- Fat: 2 g
- Protein: 6 g
- Calories: 152

Sunflower & Flax Seed Bread

Preparation Time: 10 minutes

Cooking Time: 3 hours

Servings: 10

1. Ingredients:

- 1 1/3 cup Water
- 2 tbsp butter
- 3 tbsp honey
- 1 ½ cup bread flour
- 1 1/3 cup whole wheat flour
- salt – 1 tsp
- 1 tsp active dry yeast
- ½ cup flax seeds
- ½ cup sunflower seeds

Directions:

1. Add all ingredients except for sunflower seeds into the bread machine pan.
2. Select basic setting, then select light/medium crust and press start.
3. Add sunflower seeds just before the final kneading cycle. Once loaf is done, remove the loaf pan from the machine.
4. Allow it to cool for 10 minutes. Slice and serve.

2. **Nutrition**:

- Calories: 220
- Carbs: 36.6 g
- Fat: 5.7 g
- Protein: 6.6 g

Chapter 5: Italian & French Bread

Exuberant Egg Bread

Preparation Time: 10 minutes

Cooking Time: 3 - 3½ hours

Servings: 8

Ingredients:

- ½ cup + 2 tbsp milk at 80F
- 2⅔ tbsp melted butter, cooled
- 1 whole egg, beaten

- 2⅔ tbsp sugar
- 1 tsp salt
- 2 cup white bread flour
- ¾ tsp instant yeast

Directions:

1. Add all of the ingredients to your bread machine, carefully following the instructions of the manufacturer.
2. Set the program of your bread machine to French Bread and set crust type to Light.
3. Press START.
4. Wait until the cycle completes.
5. Once the loaf is ready, take the bucket out and let the loaf cool for 5 minutes.
6. Gently shake the bucket to remove the loaf.
7. Transfer to a cooling rack, slice, and serve.

Nutrition:

- Total Carbs: 29 g
- Fiber: 1 g
- Protein: 5 g
- Fat: 5 g
- Calories: 184

Cumin Tossed Fancy Bread

Preparation Time: 10 minutes

Cooking Time: 3½ hours

Servings: 16

Ingredients:

- 5⅓ cup wheat flour
- 1½ tsp salt
- 1½ tbsp sugar
- 1 tbsp dry yeast
- 1¾ cup water
- 2 tbsp cumin
- 3 tbsp sunflower oil

Directions:

1. Add warm water to the bread machine bucket.
2. Add salt, sugar, and sunflower oil.
3. Sift in wheat flour and add yeast.
4. Set the program of your bread machine to French Bread and set crust type to Medium.
5. Press START.
6. Once the maker beeps, add cumin.
7. Wait until the cycle completes.

8. Once the loaf is ready, take the bucket out and let the loaf cool for 5 minutes.

9. Gently shake the bucket to remove the loaf.

10.   Transfer to a cooling rack, slice, and serve.

Nutrition:

- Total Carbs: 67 g
- Fiber: 2 g
- Protein: 9.5 g
- Fat: 7 g
- Calories: 368

Mesmerizing Walnut Bread

Preparation Time: 10 minutes

Cooking Time: 3 - 4 hours

Servings: 16

Ingredients:

- 4 cup wheat flour
- ½ cup water
- ½ cup milk
- 2 whole eggs, beaten
- ½ cup walnut
- 1 tbsp vegetable oil
- 1 tbsp sugar
- 1 tsp salt
- 1 tsp bread machine yeast

Directions:

1. Add milk, water, vegetable oil, and eggs to the bread maker bucket.
2. Pour in sifted wheat flour.
3. Add salt, sugar, and yeast on three sides of the bucket.

4. Set the program of your bread machine to French Bread and set crust type to Light.
5. Press START.
6. Let the kneading begin and close the lid.
7. Slightly fry the walnuts in a dry frying pan until crispy; then let them cool.
8. Once the bread maker gives the signal, add the nuts to the bread maker.
9. Mix with a spatula.
10. Let the remaining cycle complete.
11. Once the loaf is ready, take the bucket out and let the loaf cool for 5 minutes.
12. Gently shake the bucket to remove the loaf.
13. Transfer to a cooling rack, slice, and serve.

Nutrition:

- Total Carbs: 40 g
- Fiber: 1 g
- Protein: 9 g
- Fat: 7 g
- Calories: 257

Fruity French Bread

Preparation Time: 10 minutes

Cooking Time: 1 - 2 hours

Servings: 8

Ingredients:

- ¾ cup canned pears, mashed
- ¼ cup water
- 1 tbsp honey
- 1 egg, slightly beaten
- 3 cup bread flour
- 1/8 tsp pepper
- 1 tsp dry yeast

Directions:

1. Add all of the ingredients to your bread machine, carefully following the instructions of the manufacturer.
2. Set the program of your bread machine to Basic/White Bread and set crust type to Light.
3. Press START.
4. Wait until the cycle completes.
5. Once the loaf is ready, take the bucket out and let the loaf cool for 5 minutes.

6. Gently shake the bucket to remove the loaf.

7. Transfer to a cooling rack, slice, and serve.

8. Enjoy!

Nutrition:

- Total Carbs: 9 g
- Fiber: 2 g
- Protein: 5 g
- Fat: 9 g
- Calories: 158

Italian Pine Nut Bread

Preparation Time: 10 minutes

Cooking Time: 3 hours 30 minutes

Servings: 10

3. Ingredients:

- 1 cup+ 2 tbsp water
- 3 cup bread flour

- 2 tbsp sugar
- 1 tsp salt
- 1 ¼ tsp active dry yeast
- 1/3 cup basil pesto
- 2 tbsp flour
- 1/3 cup pine nuts

Directions:

1. In a small bowl, mix basil pesto and flour until well blended.

2. Add pine nuts and stir well. Add water, bread flour, sugar, salt, and yeast into the bread machine pan.

3. Select basic setting then select medium crust and press start.

4. Add basil pesto mixture just before the final kneading cycle.

5. Once loaf is done, remove the loaf pan from the machine.

6. Allow it to cool for 10 minutes. Slice and serve.

Nutrition:

- Calories: 180
- Carbs 32.4 g
- Fat 3.5 g
- Protein 4.8 g.

Chapter 6: Special Bread

Easy Bake Keto Bread

Preparation Time: 10 minutes

Cooking Time: 30 minutes

Servings: 16

Ingredients:

1. 7 whole eggs

2. 4.5 oz melted butter

3. 2 tbsp warm water

4. 2 tsp dry yeast

5. 1 tsp inulin

6. 1 pinch of salt

7. 1 tsp xanthan gum

8. 1 tsp baking powder

9. 1 tbsp psyllium husk powder

10.   2 cup almond flour

Directions:

1. Preheat the oven to 340F.

2. In a bowl, mix almond flour, salt, psyllium, baking powder, and xanthan gum.

3. Make a well in the center of the mixture.

4. Add the yeast and inulin into the center with the warm water.

5. Stir the inulin and yeast with the warm water in the center and let the yeast activate for about 10 minutes.

6. Add in the eggs and melted butter and stir well.

7. Pour the mixture into a loaf pan lined with parchment paper.

8. Allow batter to proof in a warm spot covered for 20 minutes with a tea towel.

9. Place in the oven and bake until golden brown, about 30 to 40 minutes.

10.   Cool, slice, and serve.

Nutrition:

- Calories: 140

- Fat: 13 g

- Carb: 3 g

- Protein: 3 g

Keto Bakers Bread

Preparation Time: 10 minutes

Cooking Time: 20 minutes

Servings: 12

Ingredients:

- Pinch of salt

- 4 tbsp light cream cheese, softened

- ½ tsp cream of tartar

- 4 eggs, yolks, and whites separated

Directions:

1. Heat 2 racks in the middle of the oven at 350F.

2. Line 2 baking pan with the parchment paper, then grease with cooking spray.

3. Separate egg yolks from the whites and place them in separate mixing bowls.

4. Beat the egg whites and cream of tartar with a hand mixer until stiff, about 3 to 5 minutes. Do not over-beat.

5. Whisk the cream cheese, salt, and egg yolks until smooth.

6. Slowly fold the cheese mix into the whites until fluffy.

7. Spoon a ¼ cup measure of the batter onto the baking sheets, 6 mounds on each sheet.

8. Bake in the oven for 20 to 22 minutes, alternating racks halfway through.

9. Cool and serve.

Nutrition:

- Calories: 41

- Fat: 3.2 g

- Carb: 1 g

- Protein: 2.4 g

Yeast Bread

Preparation Time: 10 minutes

Cooking Time: 4 hours

Servings: 12

Ingredients:

- 2 ¼ tsp dry yeast

- 1/2 tsp and 1 tbsp erythritol sweetener, divided

- 1 1/8 cup warm water, at 100F / 38C

- 3 tbsp avocado oil

- 1 cup / 100 grams almond flour

- ¼ cup / 35 grams oat flour

- ¾ cup / 100 grams soy flour

- ½ cup / 65 grams ground flax meal

- 1 1/2 tsp baking powder

- 1 tsp salt

Directions:

1. Gather all the ingredients for the bread and plug in the bread machine having the capacity of 2 pounds of bread recipe.

2. Pour water into the bread bucket, stir in ½ tsp sugar and yeast and let it rest for 10 minutes until emulsified.

3. Meanwhile, take a large bowl, place the remaining ingredients in it and stir until mixed.

4. Pour flour mixture over yeast mixture in the bread bucket, shut the lid, select the "basic/white" cycle or "low-carb" setting and then press the up/down arrow button to adjust baking time according to your bread machine; it will take 3 to 4 hours.

5. Then press the crust button to select light crust if available, and press the "start/stop" button to switch on the bread machine.

6. When the bread machine beeps, open the lid, then take out the bread basket and lift out the bread.

7. Let bread cool on a wire rack for 1 hour, then cut it into twelve slices and serve.

Nutrition:

- Calories: 162 Cal

- Fat: 11.3 g

- Carbohydrates: 7 g

- Protein: 8.1 g

Keto Cloud Bread Cheese

Preparation Time: 5 minutes

Cooking Time: 30 minutes

Servings: 12

Ingredients

Cream cheese filling:

- 1 egg yolk

- ½ tsp vanilla stevia drops for filling

- 8 oz softened cream cheese

Base egg dough:

- ½ tsp cream of tartar

- 1 tbsp coconut flour

- ¼ cup unflavored whey protein

- 3 oz softened cream cheese

- ¼ tsp vanilla stevia drops for dough

- 4 eggs, separated

Directions:

1. Preheat the oven to 325F.

2. Line two baking sheets with parchment paper.

3. In a bowl, stir the 8 oz cream cheese, stevia, and egg yolk.

4. Transfer to the pastry bag.

5. In another bowl, separate egg yolks from whites.

6. Add 3 oz cream cheese, yolks, stevia, whey protein, and coconut flour. Mix until smooth.

7. Whip cream of tartar with the egg whites until stiff peaks form.

8. Fold in the yolk/cream cheese mixture into the beaten whites.

9. Spoon batter onto each baking sheet, 6 mounds on each. Press each mound to flatten a bit.

10. Add cream cheese filling in the middle of each batter.

11. Bake for 30 minutes at 325F.

Nutrition:

- Calories: 120

- Fat: 10.7 g

- Carb: 1.1 g

- Protein: 5.4 g

Classic Gluten-Free Bread

Preparation Time: 5 minutes

Cooking Time: 15 minutes

Servings: 12

Ingredients:

- ½ cup butter, melted

- 3 tbsp coconut oil, melted

- 6 eggs

- 2/3 cup sesame seed flour

- 1/3 cup coconut flour

- 2 tsp baking powder

- 1 tsp psyllium husks

- ½ tsp xanthan gum

- ½ tsp salt

Directions:

1. Pour in eggs, melted butter, and melted coconut oil into your bread machine pan.

2. Add the remaining ingredients to the bread machine pan.

3. Set bread machine to gluten-free.

4. When the bread is done, remove the bread machine pan from the bread machine.

5. .Let cool slightly before transferring to a cooling rack.

6. You can store your bread for up to 3 days.

Nutrition:

- Calories: 146

- Carbohydrates 1.2 g

- Fats 14 g

- Protein 3.5 g

Gluten-Free Chocolate Zucchini Bread

Preparation Time: 5 minutes

Cooking Time: 15 minutes

Servings: 12

Ingredients:

- 1 ½ cup coconut flour

- ¼ cup unsweetened cocoa powder

- ½ cup erythritol

- ½ tsp cinnamon

- 1 tsp baking soda

- 1 tsp baking powder

- ¼ tsp salt

- ¼ cup coconut oil, melted

- 4 eggs

- 1 tsp vanilla

- 2 cup zucchini, shredded

Directions:

1. Shred the zucchini and use paper towels to drain excess water, set aside.

2. Lightly beat eggs with coconut oil, then add to bread machine pan.

3. Add the remaining ingredients to the pan.

4. Set bread machine to gluten-free.

5. When the bread is done, remove the bread machine pan from the bread machine.

6. Let cool slightly before transferring to a cooling rack.

7. You can store your bread for up to 5 days.

Nutrition:

- Calories: 185

- Carbohydrates 6 g

- Fats 17 g

- Protein 5 g

Gluten-Free Loaf

Preparation Time: 5 minutes

Cooking Time: 15 minutes

Servings: 12

Ingredients:

- ½ cup butter, melted

- 3 tbsp coconut oil, melted

- 6 eggs

- 2/3 cup sesame seed flour

- 1/3 cup coconut flour

- 2 tsp baking powder

- 1 tsp psyllium husks

- ½ tsp xanthan gum

- ½ tsp salt

Directions:

1. Pour in eggs, melted butter, and melted coconut oil into your bread machine pan.

2. Add the remaining ingredients to the bread machine pan.

3. Set bread machine to gluten-free.

4. When the bread is done, remove the bread machine pan from the bread machine.

5. Let cool slightly before transferring to a cooling rack.

6. You can store your bread for up to 3 days.

Nutrition:

- Calories: 146

- Carbohydrates 1.2 g

- Fats 14 g

- Protein 3.5 g

My Keto Bread

Preparation Time: 10 minutes

Cooking Time: 50 to 60 minutes

Servings: 6

Ingredients:

- 3 egg whites

- 1 cup of boiling water

- 2 tbsp sesame seeds

- 2 tsp cider vinegar

- 1 tsp sea salt

- 2 tsp baking powder

- 5 tbsp ground psyllium husk powder

- 1 ¼ cup almond flour

Directions:

1. Preheat the oven to 350F.

2. Mix the dry ingredients in a bowl.

3. In another bowl, add the boiling water, vinegar, and egg whites. Beat for 30 seconds with a hand mixer. Don't over mix.

4. Grease hands with oil to make 6 pieces, then arrange on a greased baking sheet.

5. Bake 50 to 60 minutes in the lower rack of the oven. Cooking Time depends on the size of the bread. The bread is ready when it makes a hollow sound when tapped.

Nutrition:

- Calories: 170

- Fat: 13 g

- Carb: 2g

- Protein: 7 g

Bread Rolls

Preparation Time: 30-45 minutes

Cooking Time: 1 hour 30 minutes

Servings: 8

Ingredients:

- 1 1/2 cup shredded mozzarella cheese, full-fat

- 2 oz cream cheese, full-fat

- 1 1/3 cup almond flour, blanched

- 2 tbsp coconut flour

- 1 1/2 tbsp baking powder

- 3 large eggs, pastured

Directions:

1. Switch on the oven, set it to 350F, and let preheat.

2. Meanwhile, stir together flours and baking powder until combined and set aside until required.

3. Place cream cheese and mozzarella cheese in a heatproof bowl, let microwave for 1 minute or until cheese melts, stirring every 30 seconds, and then let cool for 5 minutes until cool enough to handle.

4. Add flour mixture into a food processor, along with cold cheese and 2 eggs, and pulse at high speed until the dough comes together.

5. Transfer the dough onto a large sheet, cover with a plastic wrap, then knead for 3 minutes until smooth and divide it into eight sections.

6. Shape each section of dough to form a smooth ball and then place them on a baking sheet, about 2 inches apart.

7. Whisk the remaining egg, brush it generously on dough balls, and then bake in the middle rack of

the preheated oven for 21 to 23 minutes until nicely golden brown.

8. Serve hot.

Nutrition:

- Calories: 216

- Fats: 16 g

- Protein: 11 g

- Net Carb: 4 g

- Fiber: 2 g

Oopsie Rolls

Preparation Time: 30-45 minutes

Cooking Time: 1 hour 30 minutes

Servings: 6

Ingredients:

- 3 eggs, pastured, separated

- 1/8 tsp salt

- 1/8 tsp cream of tartar, full-fat

- 3 oz cream cheese, full-fat, softened

Directions:

1. Switch on the oven set it to 300 degrees F, and let preheat.

2. Meanwhile, place egg whites in a bowl, add cream of tartar, and whip until stiff.

3. Place egg yolks in another bowl, add salt and cream cheese and whisk until smooth.

4. Fold in egg whites mixture in batches until incorporated, then take a cookie sheet, line it with

parchment paper, and spoon the egg whites mixture in six mounds.

5. Flatten each mound with a spatula and bake for 30 minutes or until the loaves of bread are nicely golden brown.

6. Let the loaves of bread cool on the cookie sheet for 10 minutes, then cool completely on a wire rack and serve.

Nutrition:

- Cal 91.3

- Fats 8.1 g

- Protein 4.2 g

- Net Carb 0.8 g

- Fiber 0 g

Chapter 7: Fruity Bread and Cake

Apple Cake

Preparation Time: 25 minutes

Cooking Time: 3 hours

Servings: 10 **Servings**

Ingredients:

- ⅔ cup water

- 3 tbsp unsalted butter, softened
- 2 cup plain bread flour
- 3 tbsp granulated sugar
- 1 tsp salt
- 1 ½ tsp active dry yeast
- 1 can apple pie filling

Directions:

1. Add the ingredients into the bread machine as per the order of the ingredients listed above or follow your bread machine's instruction manual. Do not add the pie filling.

2. Select the dough setting.

3. Remove the dough and place it onto a floured surface. Cover with a cotton cloth for 15 minutes.

4. Roll the dough out into an even rectangular shape 13" x 8." Transfer this onto a greased baking tray. Fill the dough with the apple filling, running lengthwise.

5. On each 13-inch side, make cuts from filling to edge of dough at 1-inch intervals, using a sharp knife.

6. Fold ends of the dough up over the filling. Fold strips diagonally over filling, overlapping in the center and alternating sides.

7. Cover again with the cloth and allow to rest for 30 minutes or until the dough has doubled in size.

8. Preheat your oven to 375F and bake the cake for 40 minutes or until it has reached a beautiful golden color.

9. When ready, turn the apple cake out onto a drying rack and allow it to cool.

10. When cooled, dust with powdered sugar and serve.

Nutrition:

- Calories: 480
- Total fat: 10 g
- Saturated fat: 5 g
- Cholesterol: 25 mg
- Total carbohydrates: 92 g
- Dietary fiber: 3 g
- Sodium: 710 mg
- Protein: 8 g

Coffee Cake

Preparation Time: 1 hour

Cooking Time: 1 hour and 30 minutes

Servings: 1 standard cake, serves 8

Ingredients:

- Yolk of one egg
- ¾ cup whole milk
- 1 tbsp unsalted butter, melted
- 2 ¼ cup plain bread flour
- ¼ cup sugar
- 1 tsp salt
- 2 tsp active dry yeast

Ingredients for glaze topping:

- ¼ cup pecan nuts
- ¼ cup walnuts
- 1 tsp ground cinnamon
- ½ cup sugar
- 2 tbsp unsalted butter, melted

Directions:

1. Add the ingredients into the bread machine as per the order of the ingredients listed above or follow your bread machine's instruction manual.
2. Select the dough setting.

3. Prepare a 8 x 8" baking pan by greasing it.

4. When the dough cycle is finished, transfer the cake dough into the greased baking pan.

5. For the topping, glaze the two tbsp of melted butter over the top.

6. In a small mixing bowl, combine the nuts, sugar, and cinnamon and sprinkle over the top of the cake dough.

7. Cover the cake dough with a cloth and allow to rest in a warm area for 30 minutes.

8. Preheat your oven to 375F and bake the cake for 20 minutes or until it has turned a golden color.

9. When ready, turn the bread out onto a drying rack and allow it to cool and then serve.

Nutrition:

- Calories: 313.1
- Total fat: 11.1 g
- Saturated fat: 4 g
- Cholesterol: 35.9 mg
- Total carbohydrates: 48.5 g
- Dietary fiber: 2 g
- Sodium: 344.1 mg
- Protein: 5.9 g

Chapter 8: Rolls and Pizza

Low-Carb Dinner Rolls

Preparation Time: 10 minutes

Cooking Time: 10 minutes

Servings: 6

Ingredients:

- 1 cup almond flour

- ¼ cup flaxseed (ground)
- 1 cup mozzarella (shredded)
- 1 oz cream cheese
- ½ tsp baking soda
- 1 egg

Directions:

1. Preheat your oven to 400F.
2. Using a microwave-safe mixing bowl, put both the mozzarella and cream cheese. Microwave it for one minute. Stir them till they become smooth.
3. Add eggs in the bowl and stir till they mix well.
4. In another clean bowl, put your flaxseed, almond flour, and baking soda and mix the dry ingredients.
5. Pour your egg and cheese mix into the bowl with dry ingredients. Use your hand mixer or hands to make dough by kneading.
6. Slightly wet your hands with coconut oil or olive oil and roll your dough to six balls.
7. Top them with sesame seeds and place them on the parchment paper.
8. Bake them for 10 minutes. A golden-brown look will indicate that they are done.
9. Leave them to cool.

Nutrition:

- Calories: 218
- Fat: 18 g
- Saturated Fat: 5 g
- Protein: 10.7 g
- Carbohydrates: 5.6 g
- Sodium: 103 mg
- Fiber: 3.3 g
- Sugar: 3 g

Low-Carb Clover Rolls

Preparation Time: 10 minutes

Cooking Time: 20 minutes

Servings:8

Ingredients:

- 1/3 cup coconut flour or 1 1/3 cup almond flour
- 1 ½ cup mozzarella cheese (shredded)
- 1 ½ tsp baking powder
- ¼ cup parmesan cheese (grated)
- 2 oz cream cheese
- 2 eggs (large)

Directions:

1. Preheat your oven to 350F.
2. Put your almond flour and baking powder in a clean bowl and mix.
3. Using another bowl, put your mozzarella and cream cheese and microwave for a minute. Stir it well after it melts.
4. Add eggs to the cheese and stir.
5. Add the egg-cheese mix to the bowl with dry ingredients and mix thoroughly.
6. Wet your hands and knead dough into a sticky ball.

7. Put the dough ball on the parchment paper and slice into fourths.

8. Slice each fourth or quarter into 6 smaller portions.

9. Roll each small portion into balls.

10. Roll the balls into the parmesan cheese light for them to coat it.

11. Grease your 13.75" x 10.5" muffin pan and place 3 dough balls in each cup of the pan.

Nutrition:

- Calories: 283
- Fat: 18 g
- Saturated Fat: 21 g
- Protein: 17 g
- Carbohydrates: 6 g
- Sodium: 103 mg
- Fiber: 2 g
- Sugar: 1 g

Keto Bread Rolls

Preparation Time: 10 minutes

Cooking Time: 20 minutes

Servings:8

Ingredients:

- 1 1/3 cup almond flour
- 1 ½ cup shredded mozzarella cheese (part-skim)
- 2 oz cream cheese (full Fat)
- 1 ½ tbsp baking powder (aluminum-free)
- 2 tbsp Coconut flour
- 3 eggs (large)

Directions:

1. Preheat your oven to 350F.
2. In a clean bowl, put almond flour, coconut flour and baking powder. Mix well and set it aside.
3. Using a microwave-safe bowl, put the cream cheese and mozzarella in it and microwave for 30 seconds. Remove the bowl, stir and microwave again for 30 seconds. This should go on until the cheese has entirely melted.
4. Using a food processor, add the cheese, the eggs, and flour mix. Process at high speed for uniformity of the dough. (it is normally sticky.) Knead the

dough into a dough ball and separate it into 8 equal pieces. Slightly wet your hands with oil for this step.

5. Roll each piece with your palms to form a ball and place each ball on the baking sheet. (should be 2 inches apart)

6. In a bowl, add the remaining egg and whisk. Brush the egg wash on the rolls.

7. Bake for 20 minutes or until they are golden brown.

Note: the cheese hardens the rolls; thus, they should be eaten when hot. Microwave them to make soft once they cool.

Nutrition:

- Calories: 216
- Fat: 16 g
- Saturated Fat: 4 g
- Protein: 11 g
- Carbohydrates: 6 g
- Sodium: 183 mg
- Fiber: 2 g
- Sugar: 1 g

Keto Coconut Bread Rolls

Preparation Time: 10 minutes

Cooking Time: 30 minutes

Servings: 6

Ingredients:

- ½ cup coconut flour
- 4 tbsp Flaxseed (ground)
- 2 tbsp Coconut oil
- 2 tbsp Psyllium husk (powder)
- 1 tbsp baking powder
- 1 tbsp apple cider vinegar
- ¼ cup boiling water

- ½ tsp salt
- 2 egg whites
- 2 eggs (medium size)

Directions:

1. Preheat your oven to 350F.
2. In a mixing bowl, put all your dry ingredients and mix thoroughly. (Coconut flour, flaxseed flour, baking powder, psyllium husk powder, salt) add eggs and coconut oil. Blend the ingredients till it resembles breadcrumbs. Pour the apple cider vinegar and mix.
3. Add the boiling water in bits (you don't need to use the entire amount.) Stir for it to combine well with the mixture.
4. Line your baking tray with baking paper.
5. Make 6 divisions of the dough and roll them into balls with your hands.
6. Place the dough balls on the baking paper.
7. Bake them for 30 minutes or upon turning to a golden brown.

Nutrition:

- Calories: 172
- Fat: 10 g
- Saturated Fat: 2 g

- Protein: 10.7 g
- Carbohydrates: 14 g
- Sodium: 100 mg
- Fiber: 9 g
- Sugar: 1 g

Low Carb Bread Rolls (Without Eggs)

Preparation Time: 15 minutes

Cooking Time: 40 minutes

Servings:6

Ingredients:

- ¼ cup coconut flour
- 1 ¼ cup almond flour
- ¼ cup psyllium husk (ground)
- 1 cup hot water
- 1 tbsp olive oil
- 2 tsp apple cider vinegar
- 2 tsp Baking powder
- ½ tsp salt
- 2 tbsp Sesame seeds (optional)

Directions:

1. Preheat your oven to 375F.
2. Add all your dry ingredients in a bowl. (Coconut flour, almond flour, psyllium powder, baking powder, salt)
3. Pour the olive oil and apple cider vinegar into the hot water and stir. Thereafter, pour the mix into the bowl and combine thoroughly for a minute. The flour will absorb the water forming the dough. The

dough will be soft and sticky. Leave it for 10 minutes for the water mixture to be well absorbed.

4. Separate the dough into 6 equal portions. Form 6 dough balls as a result.

5. Line your baking tray with parchment paper.

6. Place the balls on the baking tray and sprinkle sesame seeds on top. Press the seeds into the dough to prevent falling out.

7. Bake for 40 minutes at 375F at the lower section of the oven for the first 30 minutes. Switch them to the top section for the remaining period.

8. Remove from the oven and let them cool.

Nutrition:

- Calories: 230
- Fat: 18 g
- Saturated Fat: 5 g
- Protein: 6.2 g
- Carbohydrates: 13.9 g
- Sodium: 132 mg
- Fiber: 9.2 g
- Sugar: 1.9 g

Chapter 9: How to Store Bread

Storing bread isn't always easy. If you manage not to eat all of the delicious goodies that you bake, you should find the best ways to store them so that you can keep them fresh longer. There are plenty of different things to keep in mind when it comes to storing bread, but homemade bread is especially delicate. Here are some tips to help you get the most out of your storage:

Dough

After the kneading cycle, remove the dough from the machine. If you plan on using the dough within three days, you can store it in the refrigerator. Form the dough into a disk and place it in a sealable freezer bag, or store the dough in a lightly oiled bowl covered with plastic wrap. Yeast action will not stop in the refrigerator, so punch the dough down until it is completely chilled, and then once a day. When you are ready to bake bread, remove the dough from the refrigerator, shape it, let it rise, and bake. Bread machine dough has no preservatives, so freeze it if you aren't baking it in three days. Form the dough into a disk and place it in a sealable freezer bag. You can freeze bread dough for up to a month. When you are ready to bake the bread, remove the dough from the freezer, store it in the refrigerator overnight, shape it, let it rise, and bake. You can shape the dough into braids, loaves, knots, or other shapes before refrigerating or freezing it. Wrap the shapes tightly and store them in the refrigerator (if you are baking within 24 hours) or the freezer. At the right time, unwrap the dough, allow it to rise at room temperature, and bake it.

Don't store bread in the refrigerator.

While this might seem like a freshness solution, it actually changes the alignment of the starch molecules, which is what causes bread to go stale. If you have leftovers from what you have baked, keep it on the counter or in the bread box.

Make sure that you don't leave bread sitting out for too long. Once you cut into a loaf, you have a limited amount of time to wrap it up and secure the freshness inside. If the interior is exposed to the air for too long, it will start to harden and go stale much quicker.

If your home or the bread itself is warm, do not put it in a plastic bag.

The warmth will encourage condensation, which will prompt mold growth in the warm, moist environment. Wait until bread cools completely before storing it.

Pre-sliced and store-bought bread are going to go bad much quicker, simply because of all of the exposure and additives (which, ironically, are sometimes to retain freshness). If you're making your own bread with your bread machine, and you manage to have leftovers, these tips will make sure that you get the most out of your bread.

Moisture Matters

Just as with the baking process, the humidity and moisture in your home will affect the lifespan of your bread. It will also affect the storage options that you have. If the weather is more humid, you could leave bread on the counter overnight. However, it may have a softer crust as a result. Too much humidity means you need to store your bread in airtight containers and remove as much air and moisture as you can before storage.

That means letting the bread cool to room temperature before putting into plastic bags or containers. You will also want to hold off on slicing your bread when it first comes out of the bread machine. Unless you are going to eat the entire loaf within a short period of time, the best plan is to wait. When you cut into warm bread, steam comes out. That steam is moisture, which is helping the bread stay fresh and delicious. If you cut it too soon, you'll lose that freshness.

If you leave bread out on the counter and it is too dry, it will quickly turn into a brick. The lack of humidity is too much for fresh bread, and even too much for most store-bought varieties. Moisture is a balance, and you have to find what works for your bread, and in your home. Remember that whole grain bread, French bread, and other harder bread will generally last much longer than soft sandwich bread.

If you store your bread in plastic too soon or for too long, the crust will go soft, as we mentioned before. However, you can avoid this by leaving the bread on the counter or wrapping it loosely with a cloth or paper once it is cool. For crust lovers, this is crucial. It's all about figuring out what works in your home and with your tastes, so feel free to experiment with storage solutions, too.

To Freeze Or Not To Freeze?

You can freeze your bread. However, you simply have to be sure that you are doing it the right way. First of all, make sure that the bread is cooled to room temperature and that you have a paper or cloth wrapped around it to help collect and retain the moisture. Seal it tightly or wrap it securely, and store away for up to six months. Ideally, use a vacuum sealer to make sure the bread is completely sealed.

The difficulty in freezing bread and other baked goods is not actually in the freezing process, but the thawing. It is critical that you take the bread out of the freezer ahead of time. Rather than defrosting it in the microwave or oven, you need to let it thaw completely. This will allow the bread to re-absorb any moisture that it lost during the freezing process, keeping it fresh and delicious. Once the bread comes to room temperature, you can toss it in the oven for a few minutes to warm it up.

Reheating bread is tricky. Moisture is the biggest problem with reheating or storing bread, and freezing can affect that in many different ways. It is going to be up to you to figure out the best ways to store and reheat your bread, but these tips should definitely help.

Other Storage Solutions

There is also the option of the bread box. Many bakers have been using these for centuries, and although they aren't as popular now as they were 20 years ago, they do still exist. Is a bread box the right choice for your bread? Consider a few things:

The type of material the box is made of. Metal versus wood boxes makes a big difference. It might also affect the storage and shelf-life based on other elements.

What type of bread are you storing? All bread are different and react differently when stored. Make sure that you take the time to get to know your bread varieties, as well as what is best for them.

Conclusion

While people love home-baked bread, some individuals don't like the smoothness of bread baked in a device, and often ignore the convenience of a bread maker to produce bread. The machine does all the kneading work on the dough system, which helps it to go through the initial cycles of rising and rest. Not only does it save energy, but it also causes a less baking mess. The dough and the basic white bread recipes can be used to make the sweet dough, pizza dough, and cinnamon bunks for some of the options.

Launching and finishing bread in a bread machine yields better results with less time than mixing by hand. Whenever the dough cycle completes, you create it for the second time and allow it to rise—Bake as you wish in the oven. By using a bread machine, you may concentrate your attention on certain household activities or meal chores when the dough process is in process. And it helps you to perform multiple tasks in a sense.

A bread machine has many benefits over conventional bread baking and purchasing the pre-packed loaves at a store. Sometimes, this is cheaper. The machines are very user friendly. You ought to be precise with the proportions. Without a bread maker, you can certainly make traditional bread, but this machine can be convenient for cleaning and preparing. You can control your bread recipes, so it is easy to adapt the recipes or ingredients accordingly if you would like gluten-free flour or reduced salt. But as gluten makes the standard bread texture, you have to ensure that you have the correct gluten-free flour and that your bread maker is "gluten-free" so that it is perfectly baked. Also, if you try to reduce the amount of palm oil, making bread on your own is a good way to do that, as many shops purchased bread contain palm oil. If you bake regularly, then buying a bread machine makes absolute sense. The gadget can make both mixing and kneading the dough simple for you. Moreover, the celebrations, occasions, and other festivals are incomplete without the bread. A variety of ingredients are added according to the occasion as well as season. Some problems with bread machines are shape issues in which the final product is asymmetrical and not enough spongy and fluffy. Issues with the texture include bread being denser, having a large number of holes, and not completely baked in a given time. Careful handling of ingredients measurement and following the suggested order for the ingredients can reduce the chances of getting a faulty loaf of bread. Careful handling of ingredients measurement and following the suggested order for the ingredients can reduce the chances of getting a faulty loaf of bread. All in all, it can be deduced that bread machine would save you a lot of time and energy to knead the dough you'd put in and you would need less workforce too if you own a venture. Hence it's economical as well.